CATHERINE THE GREAT
AND TSARSKOYE SELO

Aalborg Historical Museum

1992

Published in connection with the exhibition
"Catherine the Great and Tsarskoye Selo"
at Aalborg Historical Museum,
June 16th-August 31st 1992.

Editor and layout:
Erik Nørager Pedersen.

Photographs:
Poul Pedersen and Ole Hein Pedersen.

Printing:
Nordjyllands Bogtrykkeri.

ISBN: 87-980257-6-7

The exhibits are in the possession of
The Catherine Palace, Tsarskoye Selo,
in Pushkin near Saint Petersburg.

The exhibition and book have received
generous financial support from:
Queen Margrethe's and Prince Henrik's Foundation
Carlsbergs Mindelegat for Brygger J. C. Jacobsen
Cold Stores Foundation
Samson Transport Co.
Kay Wilhelmsen A/S
Aalborg kommune

Foreword

The exhibition, *Catherine the Great and Tsarskoye Selo* is being presented abroad for the first time.

The exhibits show the age of Catherine the Great, later known as "The Golden Age", her personality, her tastes and her attachments. Tsarskoye Selo was her favourite residence.

The many 18th century Russian watercolours show the historical places which still exist today. Among the portraits, there are some of Catherine the Great and the members of her family. Of these, the portrait of Catherine and that of her son, Paul, painted by Alexander Roslin are of great interest.

Engravings by the Russian school of the 18th century reflect the main historical events of the time of Catherine the Great, while details of court life in her time are well illustrated in the exhibition.

The collection also includes some items of porcelain made by order of Catherine II at the Gardner plant, the first Russian private factory.

Ivan P. Sautov, Director, Tsarskoye Selo

Catherine II of Russia in guards' regiment uniform riding the horse Brillante on 28 June 1762. Painting by Vigilius Erichsen. Collection of Statens Museum for Kunst, Copenhagen.

Catherine the Great and Tsarskoye Selo

L. Kanaeva, T. Stradova

The history of Tsarskoye Selo is inseparable from Catherine the Great who visited it a good deal and resided there during the fifty-odd years she lived in Russia, first as Grand Princess, the wife of the heir, then as Empress and the owner of this suburban residence. It was in Tsarskoye Selo that she spent the last summer of her life. It is no coincidence therefore that the period in the history of Tsarskoye Selo connected with Catherine the Great is called its Golden Age; in that period the Imperial residence grew and acquired the apperance it has retained up until the present day. The magnificence of Tsarskoye Selo amazes us to the same degree as it did the contemporaries of the Empress. The French diplomat, Count de Ségur, recalls in his memoirs, "When I came to Tsarskoye Selo, the Empress was kind enough to show me the beauty of her splendid suburban palace. Clear waters, shady gardens, elegant bowers, luxurious furniture and rooms faced with porphyry, lazurite and malachite – this wonderful sight made the astounded traveller think of Semiramis's palaces and gardens".

In the late eighteenth century, the last years of the reign of Catherine the Great, Tsarskoye Selo, due to its size and beauty, ranked with the most luxurious royal residences of Europe.

The history of Tsarskoye Selo begins with a small suburban manor; a lot of similar manors appeared around St. Petersburg in the early eighteenth century. Later, some of these disappeared, while others, such as Petershof, Oranienbaum and Tsarskoye Selo, grew into grandiose Imperial residences.

The first owner of Tsarskoye Selo was the wife of Peter the Great, Catherine I; the Great (Catherine) Palace built there was named after her.

No serious construction works had been carried out in Tsarskoye Selo until the 1740s, when it passed to the Empress Elizabeth who was attached to this place to no lesser degree than her mother. On her order, reconstruction and expansion of the palace was started in 1744. In the same year, the fifteen-year-old German princess, Sophie-Fredericke-Auguste of Anhalt-Zerbst came to Russia to marry Grand Prince Peter Alexeyevich (afterwards, Peter III). She embraced Orthodoxy and was baptised Catherine Alexeyevna. The Princess, who witnessed the erection of the Palace, later recalled that the construction was being supervised by the Empress herself, and if the latter was dissatisfied with something, the next day it was destroyed. "The Palace had been destroyed and rebuilt six times before it acquired its present appearance". Several architects took part in the construction which was completed by Bartolomeo Francesco Rastrelli who was also the designer of the Palace's interiors. The erection of the Palace was a noticeable event in the life of Russia. On July 30, 1756, the chief architect, Rastrelli, showed the Palace to the Empress, her Court and the diplomatic corps. The Grand Princess Catherine was also there.

The French ambassador to the Russian Court, who was in Tsarskoye Selo on that day, sent to Paris a rapturous description of the new palace in which he drew special attention to the Chinese and the Amber rooms, "astounding in their splendour and luxury". Simultaneously with the Palace, a regular park was created. In the mid-eighteenth century, Tsarskoye Selo became a baroque palace and park complex whose size and magnificence exceeded those of many similar complexes not only in Russia but also in Western Europe..

A new period in the history of Russia and Tsarskoye Selo began with the enthronement of Catherine the Great in 1762. Her reign, with both it positive and negative aspects, was one of the most outstanding epochs in Russian history and had an effect on a large number of subsequent events, as well as on the development of culture and the arts. Sensitive to the tastes of her time, Catherine became interested in classical art, which was concordant with the aesthetics of Classicism, the new style that established itself in the 1770s and 1780s. Of all the arts, her favourite was architecture. One of her contemporaries quotes her in his memoirs, "The overwhelming desire to build is a possession by the devil, to say nothing of the money it requires. But the more you build, the more you want to. It is a vice similar to dipsomania". The two passions of the Empress, her love of Classical antiquity and craving for building, were reflected in the subsequent evolution of her Tsarskoye Selo residence. She ordered reconstruction and some changes to be made in accordance with the principles of Classicism. At the time, such outstanding architects as Antonio Rinaldi, Yuri Velten, Vassily and Ivan Neyelov, Charles Cameron and Giacomo Quarenghi were working in Tsarskoye Selo. Wings were added to the Palace; new interiors were created; pavilions were erected in the park. The appearance of the park also changed. The trees and bushes in the regular part were no longer trimmed and the park came to resemble a shady garden. Near it, on the banks of the Great Pond, a landscape park was created, which was more concordant with the current taste as well as that of the Empress. In 1772, Catherine wrote to Voltaire, "I am now fond of English gardens, curves, sloping inclines, ponds like lakes, and archipelagoes on land; I hate straight lines". However, Catherine's taste was not the only thing reflected in the architecture of Tsarskoye Selo. First and foremost, she was the sovereign of a vast empire which held a noticeable place in European policy. To commemorate some of Russia's brilliant victories in the Russo-Turkish war of 1768-1774, the Empress ordered monuments to be erected in the landscape part of the park, viz. the Chesme, the Morea and the Kagoul column by Antonio Rinaldi or the Ruin Tower by Yuri Velten. "If this war continues, the Empress wrote in 1771, the garden of Tsarskoye Selo will look like a bowling-alley, for after each victory I have a new monument erected there".

The annexation of the Crimea as a result of another victory was commemorated by the Crimea Column by Yuri Velten.

According to Catherine's plan, the chief edifice of the landscape park was to be a "villa in Classical style". For this, Charles Cameron, a British architect, was commissioned. In 1780-1787, he created a complex of buildings, based on the model of Roman thermae. The buildings, which became part of the Palace ensemble, included the Cold Bath, the Agate Rooms, the Hanging Garden, the Gallery (later named after its creator) and the Ramp. Among these, especially beautiful are the Agate Rooms faced with the Urals jasper, a real masterpiece of architecture and interior decoration.

Simultaneously, Cameron created new interiors in the Catherine Palace, viz. Catherine's private rooms, those of her son, Grand Prince Paul and his wife, Maria, and the Ceremonial Rooms. In the décor of the Empress's Rooms and the Ceremonial Rooms, Cameron used very expensive facing materials, e.g. Russian semi-precious stones, while the heir's rooms were more modest, though as remarkable in the effect they produced. One of the most elaborate interiors of the Palace was that of the Lyon Room. Its name derives from the chief element of its décor, the French silk produced by Camille de Pernon's factory in Lyon, after the cartoons by Philippe de Lassalle. Besides the silk, the interior decoration contained the rare Badakhshan lazurite used in the facing of the lower part of the walls. The parquetry consisted of palisander

The Grand Duchess Catherine Aleksejevna.
Etching by E. Vinogradov, 1761. 44 × 30 cm.

7

ornamented with amaranthe, palm, black- and rosewood, with mother-of-pearl inlays.

Besides interior decoration, Catherine was regardful of the furnishing of the rooms of the Palace which, despite all its luxury, had practically no furniture when inherited by Catherine. In 1766, she wrote to one of her correspondents, "I have been here for a week, in the palace which the late Elizabeth took trouble to have gilded both within and without. Yet, it has not a comfortable armchair or even a table to lean on".

Under Catherine the Great, paintings, sculptures, furniture, porcelain, bronzes and other works of art were purchased in quantity. Painters, sculptors, and cabinet makers were working on Catherine's commissions, both in Russia and abroad. Many of these works of art, purchased specially for the Palace in Tsarskoye Selo, formed the core of its collection.

The last and most important project of Catherine the Great was the erection of the Alexander Palace designed by Giacomo Quarenghi in 1792-1796 for Catherine's favourite grandson Grand Prince Alexander (afterwards, Alexander I).

Having spent much time and effort to make life in Tsarskoye Selo comfortable for her and her associates, Catherine preferred the Palace to her other suburban residences. Therefore Tsarskoye Selo was the arena of many events that took place both in the private and official life of the Empress. It was in Tsarskoye Selo that her ceremonial entry into St. Petersburg started after the coronation in Moscow in 1763. From then on, she spent much time there almost every year, leaving Tsarskoye Selo only in the winter when she moved to the Winter Palace in St. Petersburg. To Tsarskoye Selo,

the news of one of Russia's most glorious victories in the Turkish war, the battle of Kagoul, was brought. In Tsarskoye Selo Catherine preferred to celebrate her birthday (April 21), as well as those of her family. In Tsarskoye Selo her grandsons, Constantine and Nicholas (afterwards, Nicholas I), were born. But Tsarskoye Selo knew not only rejoicing. It was here that Catherine had to live through the untimely death of her favourite, Lanskoy, whose statue was erected in the park.

Catherine the Great shared the time she spent in Tsarskoye Selo between matters of state (usually in the morning) and entertainments (in the evening). One of the visitors to Tsarskoye Selo describes it as follows, "Her Majesty was busy throughout the morning, during which time each of us could read, write, walk, in a word, do whatever he or she liked. At dinner, there were few people and few courses; the food was good, but simple, without any luxury. The time after dinner was devoted to games and conversations". It was the Empress's habit, having finished with state matters, to spend time among the visitors she invited to Tsarskoye Selo. As one of them, Count de Ségur, recalled, "With the absolute freedom, the gaiety of conversation and no boredom at all, it was the magnificent palace alone that reminded me that the place where I was, was not the country house of my sweetheart, a woman of society. Cobenzl was invariably merry, Fitz-Herbert demonstrated his learning and intelligence, Potyomkin, his originality which never deserted him, even at the moments of melancholy or depression. The Empress talked freely about everyting except politics; she liked to listen to stories, and she liked to tell stories too". Every day Catherine

Vigilius Erichsen: Catherine II of Russia in coronation robes, 1767. Her Majesty Queen Margrethe's collection at Amalienborg Palace.

The coronation of Catherine II in the Uspenski Cathedral in the Kremlin, 22 September 1762. Etching by A. Kazachinsky. 47 × 71 cm.

Coronation banquet in the Granovit Chamber in the Kremlin, 22 September 1762. Etching by A. Kazachinsky. 47 × 71 cm.

walked in the park, accompanied by her grandchildren and courtiers. When the weather was bad, she preferred to walk in the Cameron Gallery. She also spent much time in the Agate Rooms where she read; therefore her favourite books from the Imperial Library were brought there. In this and other rooms of the Palace, here and there, were snuffboxes. The Empress used a sort of tobacco grown specially for her in Tsarskoye Selo.

According to the *Court Journal,* which recorded all the events that took place at the Court, assemblies, balls, masquerades and gala dinners were held in the Ceremonial Rooms, the most important of these taking place in the Grand Room of the Palace. There was probably no sovereign who visited Tsarskoye Selo without a ceremonial dinner being given in his or her honour in the Grand Room. Especially remarkable was the dinner given in honour of Joseph II of Austria on June 18, 1780. At the dinner on July 6, 1790, the day Grand Prince Nicholas, Catherine's grandson was baptised, 174 persons were present. In the same room a masquerade was held in 1770, on the occasion of the visit of Prince Henry of Prussia. The masquerade was accompanied by illuminations along the entire road between Tsarskoye Selo and St. Petersburg and ended in wonderful fireworks which were an indispensable part of all the festivals in Tsarskoye Selo. Illuminations, music and fireworks made the festival look like theatre performances. Especially spectacular were the fireworks on the Great Pond in front of the Catherine Palace.

Small soirées and card games were held, as a rule, in the Jasper Room where the Empress also received foreign ambassadors.

In between official galas, smaller parties and balls took place, when some of the men wore women's clothes "for amusement". The courtiers also took part in amateur performances.

The significance of Tsarskoye Selo as an Imperial residence did not change until the beginning of the twentieth century.

Today Tsarskoye Selo is an important museum of history and the arts, whose collection includes some twenty thousand items. The most valuable portion of this collection dates from the eighteenth century. Some of its paintings, drawings, sculptures and works of decorative and applied arts are represented in the exhibition, *Catherine the Great and Tsarskoye Selo*. Besides their value as works of art, the exhibits are of great historical importance, for they help us reconstruct one of the most interesting periods in the history of Russia, the reign of Catherine the Great.

One of the exhibits, an etching by Grigory Kachalov (1711/12-1759), shows fireworks on the

Fireworks, 24 November 1773 on the occasion of Catherine II's day of christening. Etching by M. Nemov. 26 × 36 cm.

Theatre performance at San Bernedetto in honour of Grand Duke Paul Petrovitsch and Grand Duchess Maria Fedorovna, 22 january 1782. Etching by A. Barotti. 42 × 59 cm.

Neva, St. Petersburg, on the occasion of the wedding of Princess Catherine and Grand Prince Peter (afterwards, Peter III) in 1745.

One of the earliest portraits of Catherine as Russian Grand Princess was made by Pietro Rotari. The collection of Tsarskoye Selo has a rare etching after it, by two outstanding engravers of the Engraving Department of the Academy of Science, Ivan Sokolov and Efim Vinogradov (the latter completed the engraving after Sokolov's death). The portrait was created in 1761.

In 1762, as a result of the overthrow of Peter III, Catherine became the Empress of Russia. The copy of the painting by Stefano Torelli and three

etchings after the drawings by Jean-Louis Develly (1730?-after 1780) and Mikhail Makhayev (ca. 1717-1770), from the Coronation Album, show some of the episodes of the Coronation that took place in the Dormition Cathedral in Moscow. By tradition, the coronation was to be held in Moscow, the old capital of Russia. In the Dormition Cathedral of the Kremlin, all the patriarchs were ordained and all the monarchs crowned beginning with John IV the Terrible. The first Imperial coronation in Russia was that of Catherine I, wife of Peter the Great, on May 7, 1724.

The copy of Torelli's painting shows Catherine II adopting the Crown and the Gown of the Russian Empress. The ceremony was accompanied by the singing of hymns, artillery salvoes and bells tolling.

The etchings show (1) preparations for the exit from the Cathedral after the coronation, the Divine Liturgy, chrismation at the Tsar Gate and communion at the altar; (2) dinner in the Faceted Chamber of the Kremlin; and (3) reception of ambassadors by the new Empress.

The art of bone carving, traditional in the North of Russia, flourished in the seventeenth and eighteenth centuries when carving workshops appeared in Moscow and St. Petersburg. The products of these workshops are represented by a relief depiction of Catherine the Great with the attributes of her Imperial power, the gown and laurels, or the portraits of the sovereigns of Russia, from Riurik to Alexander I. It should be noted that the portrait of Catherine II follows that of Elizabeth, which conveys the idea of the direct succession of power, inherited, as it were, by the princess of an insignificant German duchy; no portrait of her husband, Peter III, is represented here. The same idea is present in the carved cup with portraits of three emperors, Pavel Petrovich, Peter's daughter Elizabeth, and Catherine the Great.

A number of plans and ideas later to be implemented were conceived in Tsarskoye Selo. One of them, the *Instruction for the Commission for the Preparation of the New Code of Laws* became the symbol of the Empress's policy of reforms. The collection of Tsarskoye Selo has a rare edition of this book, printed in 1770 in St. Petersburg.

As a result of the victory in the first Russo-Turkish war, Russia established herself on the Black Sea. The peace signed with Turkey was celebrated in July 1775. Two etchings, by M. Kazakov and S. Fedoseyev, showing fireworks on the Khodynka Field, commemorate this event.

The glorious victory of the Russian fleet led by Count Orlov is depicted on the Chesme Vase produced in the 1780s by the Imperial Porcelain Works. One of the medallions shows Orlov wearing armour, the inscription reads, "Count A. S. Orlov, the victor and the destroyer of the Turkish fleet"; another, inscribed "Russia rejoiced again... November 13, 1771", shows the sea battle.

In the context of the Russo-Turkish wars and, more generally, Catherine's policy, Prince Grigory Potyomkin should be mentioned. His portrait was executed by the outstanding Russian sculptor Fedot Shubin in 1791. Potyomkin, Catherine's favourite, was a statesman, a participant in the Russo-Turkish wars and the author of the project to organize Little Russia (Ukraine), of which he was the Governor-General. Potyomkin was responsible for the foundation of Sebastopol and Ekaterinoslav (Novorossiysk) and the creation of the Black Sea fleet, as well as the "Greek project" for the destruction of the Ottoman Empire. He was one of the most outstanding personalities of his time.

Also by Shubin is the sculptural portrait of Catherine with laurels (1780s).

For the participants in the Russo-Turkish wars, the Empress established the Order of St. George (November 26, 1769) which later became the most honourable Russian order. It was awarded "For Service and Valour". The Orders of other saints were also established. On the days of the patron saints, the so called "Order Ceremonies" were held in Tsarskoye Selo, with the participation of the knights of the respective Order. For these ceremonies, the Gardner Porcelain Works (the oldest in Russia; founded 1767) in the village of Verbilki near Moscow, made "Order Sets"; items from two of these, St. George (1778) and St. Vladimir (1783-1785), are shown in the exhibition.

A miniature by an unknown artist, after the painting by Rokotov, shows Catherine wearing the insignia of the Order of St. George. The inscriptions on the ribbon on the wreath-frame remind one of some of the events of Catherine's reign: the division of Poland in 1794, the annexation of Tauride (the Crimea) in 1783 and the Province of Kuban in 1787. Below, are the dates of Catherine's reign: 1762-1796.

In Tsarskoye Selo, ceremonies devoted to the Guards Regiments were held, where the Empress appeared wearing a "uniform dress" which corresponded to the uniform of the respective regiment. The collection of Tsarskoye Selo has a rare Horse Guards Uniform Robe that belonged to Catherine the Great.

Under Catherine, furniture, paintings and tapestries were acquired for the palaces and pavilions of Tsarskoye Selo. Some of these were purchased abroad; others, of an equally high quality, were commissioned from Russian artists and craftsmen, e.g. the table with marquetry and bronze inlays or the tapestry after the cartoon by Iogann Friedrich Groot, the author of many animalistic paintings, produced by St. Petersburg Tapestry Works, the purveyor to the Russian Court.

Some of the painters were honoured by commissions to depict Tsarskoye Selo. These views still embellish the interiors of the Palace; among them are four paintings by Gerard Delabarthe (de

Cornelius Høyer: Catherine II.
Pencil drawing on paper, April 1782.
Study for miniature on ivory.
Collection of "Kobberstiksamlingen", Copenhagen.

la Barthe) who worked in Moscow and St. Petersburg in 1787-1810. The four paintings (two of them shown in the present exhibition) were produced in 1787; the painter was paid 1,200 roubles, a lot of money at the time, which suggests that the Empress was satisfied. The paintings, *Lake in Tsarskoye Selo* and *View of Catherine Park*, show Tsarskoye Selo as it was in the time of Catherine, i.e. the time of its flourishing. In the *Lake in Tsar-*

skoye Selo, one can see the Grotto Pavilion in the Russian Baroque style, designed by Rastrelli and built in 1749-1770, and, in the distance, the airy Cameron Gallery built in 1783-1786.

The beautiful views of Tsarskoye Selo attracted the world famous landscape painter, Hubert Robert (1733-1808) whose *œuvre* is well represented in Russia due to his popularity with the Russian nobility. His ability to combine fantasy and reality, Romanticism and elegant *chinoiserie* took Catherine's fancy and she decided to invite Robert to Russia. It was her usual practice to have poets, artists and scholars work in Russia. The persons invited were paid generously, but Robert, who was at the peak of his popularity in France, declined the invitation. Yet, he painted for the Empress the picture *Ruin Tower in Tsarskoye Selo,* based on the drawing he received through Count Stroganoff. The romantic scenery appealed to Robert. Nonetheless, he gave free rein to his fantasy: the painting shows hills in the background, though the locality never had hills; the spruces resemble trees in Chinese paintings; the peasants remind one of vaudeville characters. The Ruin Tower shown in the picture was built in 1771 from the design by Yuri Velten, to commemorate the beginning of the Turkish war in 1768.

Views of Tsarskoye Selo by Mikhail Ivanov (1748-1823) are done in water colour, a technique much favoured and well developed in Russia. Ivanov travelled a lot in the retinue of Prince Potyomkin, depicting Russian landscapes. In Tsarskoye Selo, his brush depicted the Bowed Bridge by Vassily Neyelev (1774), the Cameron Gallery, the so-called Grand Caprice in the Chinese style, designed by Neyelov and built, in 1772-1774, by I. Ge-

rard, and the Tower Bridge or Red Cascade (1779-1781). Besides their artistic value, the watercolours are an important historical record showing the minute details of the scenery as it looked at the time. For instance, the *Grand Caprice* watercolour shows, besides the Orlov Gate by Rinaldi erected in 1772 to commemorate Orlov's activities during the 1771 plague in Moscow, the buildings located towards Gatchina, and the mill, now destroyed, which gives the landscape a somewhat Dutch air. The figures demonstrate clothes worn by people who, at the time, were admitted to the park.

Since everything French was in vogue in Russia in the eighteenth century, French goods, such as clothes, fans, snuff-boxes, miniatures in the style of Boucher and Watteau, and the like were bought in quantity. It is not impossible that some of the bric-a-brac things shown at the present exhibition were, once, in the hands of Catherine the Great who used a fan and a snuff-box, as was customary at the time.

The tradition of carrying miniature portraits also became widespread. The genre itself found very favourable conditions in Russia where the art of enamelling was flourishing both in St. Petersburg and many provincial towns.

Not only goods but also styles came to Russia from France, e.g. Classicism which manifested itself in the interiors of the Palace in Tsarskoye Selo: all its chandeliers are of French work; also, the porcelain produced by the Imperial Porcelain Works in St. Petersburg (now M. V. Lomonosov Porcelain Factory), e.g. Censer Vase with Three Graces, is in the style of early Classicism. (The Imperial Porcelain Works, second only to Meissen in

Catherine II.
Marble bust by F. Schubin. 1780.
68 × 40 cm.

Grigorij Potemkin.
Marble bust by F. Schubin. 1791.
73 × 54 cm.

Europe, were founded in 1745 by D. I. Vinogradov, a chemist and creator of Russian porcelain).

M. Nemov's etching *Fireworks on November 24, 1773, the Day of Catherine II's Patron Saint* depicts one of the brilliant festivals held in Tsarskoye Selo on such occasions. In the centre is Catherine's cypher with the Imperial crown above it; under the cypher is the Coat of Arms of Tsarskoye Selo. Two triumphal columns, inscribed: *at sea* (left) and *on land* and a pile of defeated enemies' arms in the foreground remind one of Russia's victories. The inscription above reads, *Comme Votre nom est terrible à tous Vos ennemis / Ainsi il est aimé de Vos sujets et de Vos amis* (Your name that fear to your foe lends / Is loved by all your subjects and your friends).

Tsarskoye Selo was the place where Catherine used to spend time in the family circle. This tradition was started by another empress, Elizabeth, who took her grandson, Grand Prince Paul (afterwards, Paul I) to stay with her there. In his later years, however, Paul avoided Tsarskoye Selo, because of his strained relations with his mother, Catherine II. Yet, his ties with the place were strong enough, and he deserves to be represented in the present exhibition. One of the two portraits shown here, by the brilliant Swedish portrait painter Alexander Roslin (1728-1793), depicts Paul as a twenty-three-year-old Grand Prince.

Catherine was very particular about choosing a wife for the heir; it was her decision that Sophie-Dorothy, Princess of Württemberg became Grand Princess in 1776. With Orthodoxy, she adopted the name, Maria Fyodorovna. The mother of two Emperors, Alexander I and Nicholas I, she is depicted in the portrait by an unknown artist, a copy after the work by the Austrian painter Lampi, popular with the Russian Court.

Two of Catherine's grandsons, Alexander and Constantine, her favourites, lived in Tsarskoye Selo under the supervision of their grandmother who based their education on the ideas of Locke and Montaigne. Her plan was to make Alexander the Emperor of Russia, instead of his father Paul, and Constantine, the Emperor of the new Byzantine Tsardom which she hoped to create after the defeat of the Ottoman Empire (the so-called "Greek Project" by Prince Potyomkin). She commissioned a sculptural portrait of the two princes from the best Russian sculptor Fedot Shubin (1740-1805). The portrait was made in 1782.

Catherine was also very particular about her eldest grandson's marriage, choosing, as his wife, Louise-Marie-Auguste of Baden-Durlach, who became Grand Princess Elizabeth Alexeyevna. As Grand Princess, she is depicted in the portrait by an unknown painter of Levitsky's circle, a copy after the painting by Marie-Louise Vigée-Lebrun who was working in Russia in 1795-1801.

Authors of memoirs note that, whatever the circumstances, Catherine almost never deviated from her habit, almost a ritual, of taking a promenade in the parks of Tsarskoye Selo, which is depicted in the etching by Damame-Dematrais (1763-1827) after his own drawing. A pupil of David, he lived in Russia, making views of parks and palaces, as well as portraits of peasants and townpeople, collected in the albums which he published in Paris, e.g. *Collection complete de divers jardins et points de vues de maisons de plaisance imperiales de Russie* (Paris, 1811). The present work belongs to the Views of Russia series; it shows the many details of the irregular, landscape part of the Catherine Park as it was at the time of Catherine the Great, the side façade of the Zubov Annex of the Catherine Palace and the now no longer extant pavilion in place of the ramp of the Cameron Gallery. Worthy of note is the Empress's attire; Catherine is known to have disliked dresses with narrow bodices, therefore her dress, somewhat loose, looks like one typical of the early nineteenth century.

The last to be mentioned, but in no way the least, is one of the most brilliant portraits of Catherine the Great painted by Alexander Roslin, a replica of Fyodor Rokotov's work now in the Russian Museum, St. Petersburg. In a very refined manner the artist depicts the great Empress to whom Tsarskoye Selo owes so much of its beauty and glory.

Catherine II. Painting by Alexander Roslin, 1776-77, 262 × 195 cm.

Catherine II, 1790s.
Miniature portrait after a painting by Rokotov. 6.5 cm.

Catherine II. Painting by Rokotov, 1770s. 85 × 68 cm.

Grand Duke Paul Petrovitsch, son of Catherine II.
Painting by Alexander Roslin, 1777. 80 × 63 cm.

Grand Duchess Maria Fedorovna, wife of Paul I.
Painting after Johann Lampi, ca. 1780. 70 × 54 cm.

*Grand Duchess Elisabeth Aleksejevna, wife of Alexander I.
Painting after Vigée-Lebrun, 1790s. 73 × 60 cm.*

Cup with lid, carved in bone, 1780s. 34 cm high.
With portraits of Empress Elisabeth, Catherine II and Paul I.

Catherine II.
Relief portrait in ivory, ca. 1770. 6 × 4 cm.

Catherine II's uniform dress, 1766.

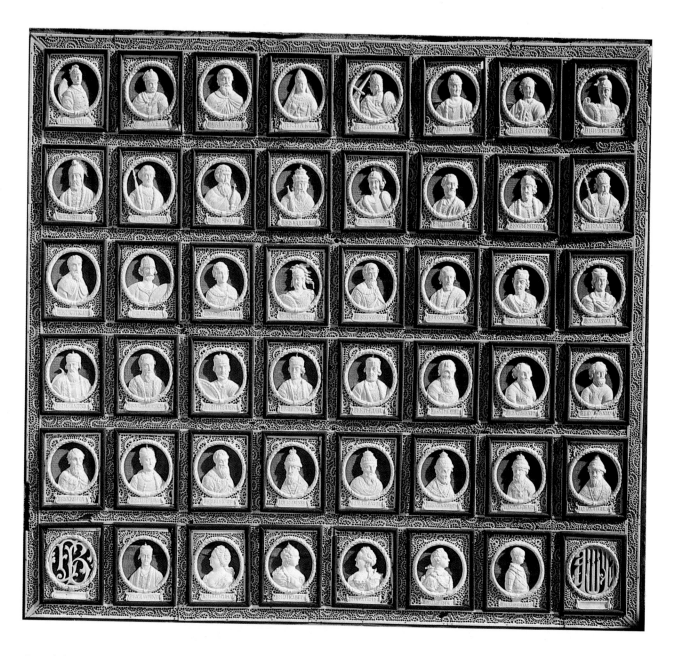

Panel showing Russian grand dukes and tsars.
The four latter are Elisabeth, Catherine II, Paul I and Alexander I.
Carved in walrus ivory, ca. 1790. 59 × 64 cm.

Section of the panel.
Bottom row: Elisabeth, Catherine II and Paul I.

The coronation of Catherine II in the Uspenski Cathedral in the Kremlin.
Painting by Guleljmi after S. Torelli, ca. 1770. 93 × 142 cm.

View of Catherine Park in Tsarskoye Selo with Cameron Gallery.
Painting by Gerard Delabarthe, 1788. 47 × 61.5 cm.

Ruin Tower in Tsarskoye Selo.
Painting by Hubert Robert, 1783. 69 × 84.5 cm.

Lake at Tsarskoye Selo.
Painting by Gerard Delabarthe, 1788. 48 × 62 cm.

*Fan of bone and paper.
Made in France,
18th century.
28 × 51 cm.*

*Tobacco case
in enamel and
mother-of-pearl.
Made in France,
18th century.
7.5 × 5.5 cm.*

China plate from the St. George set.
Made at the Gardner factory, 1777. 24.5 cm.

China bowl from the St. Vladimir set.
Made at the Gardner factory, 1782-84. 25.5 cm.

Biscuit basket of china from the St. George set.
Supplementary edition from the Lomonsov factory, 1889. 32 cm.

Triple candlestick.
Made in France, 1770s. 64 cm.

Candlestick for twelve candles.
Made in France, 1790s. 84 cm.

THE CATHERINE PALACE AT TSARSKOYE SELO

The Cameron Gallery.
Architect: Charles Cameron,
1780-85.

The Upper Baths Pavilion
with the Agate Room.
Architects: Ivan Neyelov
and Charles Cameron,
1777-79.

The Formal Staircase in the Catherine Palace by I. Monighetti, 1861.

*The Great Hall
in the Catherine Palace
Architect: Rastrelli,
1750s.*

*The Pilaster Room.
Architect: Rastrelli,
1750s.*

The Hall of Paintings.
Architect: Rastrelli,
1750s.

The Butler's Room.
Architect: Vasily Stasov,
1840s.

The Formal Bedroom.
Architect: Charles Cameron,
1780s.

The Green Dining Room.
Architect: Charles Cameron,
1780s.

View of the park at Tsarskoye Selo from the Cameron Gallery.